ICE KITCHEN

50 LOLLY RECIPES

Sensations on a stick

Cesar and Nadia Roden

Photography by Adam Slama
Illustrations by Peter Roden & Divya Scialo

Quadrille
PUBLISHING

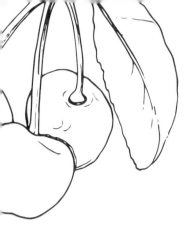

Publishing Director: Jane O'Shea
Creative Director: Helen Lewis
Senior Editor: Céline Hughes
Designers: Peter Roden, Gemma Hogan
Production: Vincent Smith, Sasha Hawkes

First published in 2014 by
Quadrille Publishing Limited
Alhambra House
27-31 Charing Cross Road
London WC2H 0LS
www.quadrille.co.uk

Cataloguing in Publication Data: a catalogue record for
this book is available from the British Library.

ISBN: 978 184949 466 3

Printed in China

CONTENTS

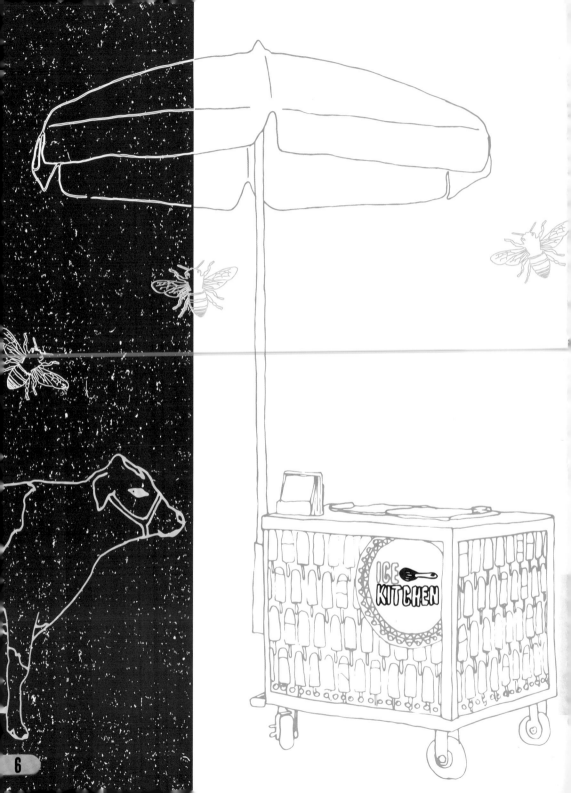

GOOD GOLLY, 50 LOLLIES!

Ice Kitchen was launched in London in spring 2013 with the aim of selling gourmet artisan ice lollies. After a fantastic summer on the street, we continued to experiment and explore the endless possibilities of an ice lolly. This is a collection of our favourite recipes that can easily be made at home and that you can enjoy throughout the year on every kind of occasion.

On the following pages you will find our aunt and nephew story, from its beginning in New York to the streets of London.

Be sure to take a look at the Techniques section before you start on your ice lolly journey - there are lots of useful tips!

LOLLY HEAVEN,
FROM NY TO LONDON

In the summer of 2009, in Woodstock NY, I came across a photo of a transparent lolly with a leaf frozen inside it. It looked so beautiful and it immediately sparked my imagination, which started running wild with all sorts of flavours and concoctions that could be frozen in ice. I thought it was such a playful and unique idea and I couldn't help myself from pursuing it. I'm an artist and always open to new ideas; I can also get a little obsessed!

While my two-year-old daughter Lily slept, I filled sketchbooks with ideas for flavour combinations and turned our kitchen into a lab. I filled our SoHo loft with freezers and a special machine from Latin America and experimented with all sorts of flavours and textures. The challenge was how to get the best out of each ingredient, to allow its natural characteristics to shine in ice. I found that often the pairing of two flavours could bring out the best in both and I was particularly happy when I found simple combinations that worked, like oranges and lemons, or milk and honey. Herbs and spices could complement and add complexity to a fruit, like basil with cantaloupe melon, or star anise with grapefruit. A touch of lemon or lime often intensified the flavour. I was also inspired by childhood favourites that my mother Claudia (Cesar's grandmother) had made, like a pistachio and rose milk pudding, which I reconstructed as a lolly; others were inspired by classics from around the world, like the Spanish sherry with raisin, or the Sicilian cassata.

I enrolled in an ice cream university course and kept the lolly plan a secret. I found a beautiful stainless steel street cart and painted on it black and white polka dots and a 1920s flapper called Lily Lolly, running with a bunch of lollies: she represented a free spirit, which is what this endeavour felt like to me. I called the business Lily Lolly's Ice Kitchen. My stepmother, Peggy, who lives in New York, was such a big help all along the way, getting all the licences and the commercial kitchen and finding us our launch spot at Herald Square, right next to Macy's.

Our first spot at Herald Square was a disaster! The crowds were too thick and we had to push our heavy cart 25 blocks to and from our kitchen through heavy traffic in 100°F heat every day! Our first customer was a police car - we thought he'd stopped to tell us off but it was to buy a lolly. Then, another time, four police cars stopped at Herald Square and took our cart away with a crane to the police station. It was a mistake of course! But all our lollies melted in the meantime.

I was relieved and overjoyed when my nephew Cesar then arrived from London to help me. Apart from being a whizz at the cart, he has amazing taste and we worked together in the kitchen. After being offered a spot at the weekly Bryant Park Film Festival, word started to spread and the High Line Park, an overhead railway line transformed into a park in the sky above Manhattan, called us to ask for our cart! A great mix of people passed by every day and it was surreal to see so many of them holding our lollies as they strolled along the amazing garden, and wonderful to see the reactions as they tasted them. The queues at our cart were now winding along the promenade!

Cesar and I kept coming up with new flavours and to keep up with the huge demand on the High Line, I spent months in the kitchen often up until midnight. Then, unfortunately, Cesar was unable to extend his visa and had to return to London.

The next summer I put the project on ice - I wanted to devote more time to my daughter Lily. She would only be this young once and I didn't want to miss all the precious summertimes with her. Meanwhile, Cesar was sure the gourmet lollies would work as well in London despite the British weather. So when he called to say he was ready, I was very excited and sent him our cart, the blast freezer and some recipes. He named it simply Ice Kitchen and his brother Peter designed the new graphics and logo; mine had been too feminine with the polka dots and flapper and all! I'm blown away by Cesar's vision and what he's achieved with Ice Kitchen in its first summer in London. I'm so proud of him!

This book is a collaboration and a collection of recipes from the New York and London experiences plus many more we created during a winter of experimenting and testing.

ICE KITCHEN IS BORN

I started my first food venture with my school friend Liam. We sold coffee, chocolate and ice cream at various markets around London from our three-wheeled Piaggio coffee van. It was a great experience but in the end we didn't get the best spots and we ended up selling the van.

After returning from New York I really wanted to show London the special gourmet lollies, as I knew nobody else was making them like this, and I hoped this would make it easier to get the market pitches and events. I turned the upstairs kitchen of my parents' house into the Ice Kitchen with the specialist equipment Nadia had sent, and immediately started experimenting. I kept thinking of the crazy amount of labour that had been involved in New York: cooking, churning, swirling, dipping in chocolate, sprinkling with nuts, wrapping, labelling and packing. But I was eager to get out and show London how good a lolly could be! Eventually, the whole house was filled with freezers and carts and crates of fruit and I was driving my parents crazy!

My first event was on the South Bank on the Easter weekend, and it started snowing. I only sold ten lollies, and most people laughed

as I stood there shivering, trying not to scare off potential customers. I wondered if I'd made the right decision, but luckily the weather turned into one of the hottest summers on record and I started coming home with an empty cart and a sun tan!

Eating in the street has become so popular and streetfood culture and events have become huge in London. I joined Kerb, a collective of streetfood traders that 'make cities taste better' by popping up at locations around London and by hosting events of their own. They are really supportive, with a genuine community vibe that cares about good food. I love being a part of the streetfood community and the instant feedback you get from the customers!

My best pitch is at the South Bank Real Food market; I think there's no better place to be on a summer evening, enjoying a mojito lolly as you walk by the river.

I had fun working with Nadia in the kitchen - she is a real ice wizard at creating imaginative lollies! This book truly was a family affair and we've been so lucky to have so many creative family members on board. My brother Peter designed the cover and artwork along with his girlfriend Divya whose illustrations are throughout, and our friend Adam stepped in to photograph every one of the lollies. Our families have loved all of the recipes in this book and we hope you will too.

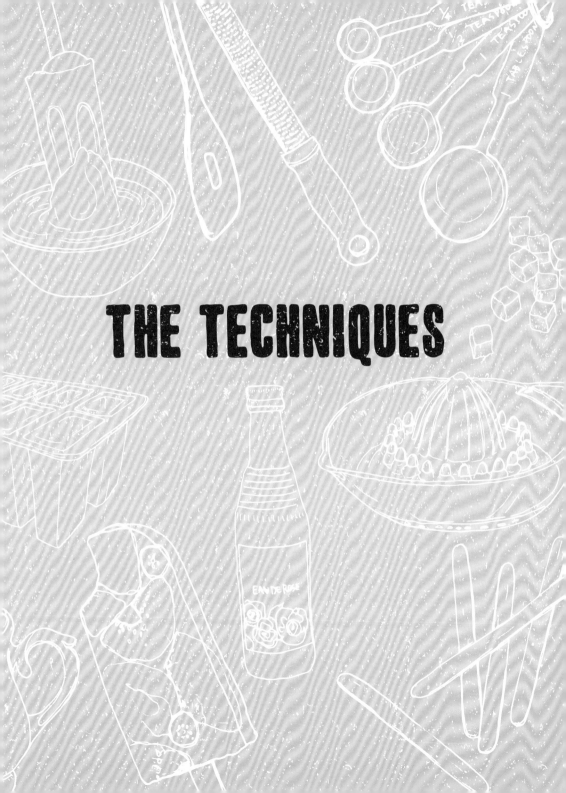

THE TECHNIQUES

THE BASICS
PROPERTIES OF AN ICE LOLLY

A pinch of salt can enhance the flavour, even for a fruit lolly.

Lolly mixtures are not churned like in ice creams or sorbets, so their texture is icy and melts quickly in your mouth.

Freezing diminishes sweetness, so make your mixture a little sweeter than you might like. We usually use natural granulated sugar but other sweeteners such as brown sugar, honey, agave syrup, maple syrup or Stevia all work fine. Syrups and honeys make smoother, softer lollies.

A tiny amount of alcohol gives a nice soft texture but too much prevents the lolly from freezing, as it has a low freezing point (2-5 tablespoons per 10 lollies is sufficient). One great idea is to dip lollies in alcohol, e.g. rum, vodka, Campari, gin or whisky.

Choose the freshest, ripest seasonal fruits. We use a touch of lemon or lime in almost all our fruity lollies as it heightens the flavour. When using citrus zest, use a fine zester and zest only the coloured part of the peel, avoiding the bitter white pith.

Infusing a base syrup with herbs and spices can complement and add complexity to different fruits. However, spices taste spicier when frozen, so use a light touch.

Use fresh whole milk, cream and yoghurt as well as good-quality chocolate, tea, nuts, herbs, spices and flowers.

TOOLS YOU'LL NEED

Kitchen scales

Strong blender or
food processor to
purée fruit

Measuring spoons

Fine-mesh sieve to
strain out solids,
such as seeds

Small or medium
saucepan to make
simple syrups, cook
fruit or heat milk

Juicer for juicing
lemons and oranges

Chopping board and knife
for cutting up fruit,
nuts and chocolate

Fine zester for zesting
lemon and orange peel

Ice-lolly mould
(see page 18)

Ice-lolly sticks

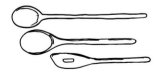

Heatproof spatula
or wooden spoon for
stirring a mixture
over heat or through
a sieve

17

THE FUN PART

FUN WITH MOULDS

There are many ready-made moulds to choose from in different shapes and sizes, and made from plastic, metal or silicone. For all the recipes in this book, a 10 x 2.5-oz. (70-ml) lolly mould was used and yielded 8-10 lollies. You can also buy expensive lolly makers that will freeze a lolly in just 15 minutes. Be creative and use other containers as moulds, such as small wax-lined paper cups, shot glasses, tall thin glasses or even ice-cube trays. Just make sure that the top of the mould isn't narrower than the bottom otherwise you won't be able to pull the frozen lolly out!

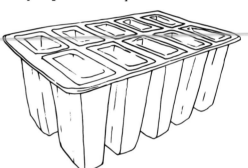

FUN WITH STICKS

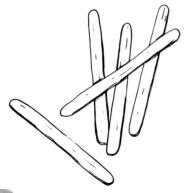

Wooden sticks are the best, as the lolly will stick firmly to them. You should buy them in large quantities - they're cheap and you'll have lots on hand. You can also be inventive and use clean twigs, bamboo or cinnamon sticks, and even a toothpick in an ice-cube tray will work. To keep the sticks in place, it's a good idea to cover the tops of the moulds with foil and cut a little slit where you want the stick, then insert the stick through the foil.

STRIPES & SWIRLS

To layer flavours in stripes, simply
part-freeze the first layer before
adding the next, and so on. It takes
a little extra time (you should wait
at least 30-60 minutes per layer) but
it's fun for a special occasion. Add
the stick after the second or third
layer. To create an angled stripe,
just prop your mould up on a bag of
frozen peas so the mixture inside
freezes at an angle and people will
wonder how you did it!

To make swirls, pour alternate layers
of two thick mixtures, or of one
thin and one thick mixture into the
mould and swizzle it a little with a
lolly stick before freezing.

SUSPENDING INGREDIENTS

Chunks of fruit, little berries, nuts,
chocolate pieces, edible flowers, herbs and
many other ingredients can be suspended
in a lolly if the mixture is thick. If the
mixture is thin, fill the mould halfway
and freeze it a little before mixing in the
suspended ingredient - this will prevent it
from sinking to the bottom. You can even
skewer some ingredients onto the sticks as
a hidden surprise.

DECORATIONS & SPRINKLES

● Place coconut flakes, chopped nuts, seeds or biscuit crumbs onto a plate or in a communal bowl on the table and roll and press the frozen lollies into them.

● Sprinkle ground spices, such as cinnamon, cayenne or cocoa onto the frozen lollies.

● To coat a lolly in chocolate, make sure the lolly is frozen hard. Put 100g chocolate and 1 tablespoon vegetable or coconut oil (the oil prevents the chocolate from cracking when frozen) in a heatproof bowl set over a saucepan of gently simmering water. Stir the chocolate until melted and smooth (and stir in chopped nuts or coconut or flavourings such as orange zest at this stage if you like). Remove from the heat and allow to cool to room temperature. To coat a lolly in chocolate, make sure the lolly is frozen hard before dipping it in. You can refreeze it on waxed paper until firm, or eat it straightaway.

● To coat a lolly in toasted nuts, preheat the oven to 180°C/350°F. Spread nuts or coconut (desiccated or flaked) on a baking tray and toast, turning with a spoon once or twice, for up to 10 minutes until lightly tanned. Cool and chop if needed.

SERVING SUGGESTIONS

You may want to make an impression with how you serve your lollies for a special occasion. They look beautiful served on a tray of ice cubes or cracked ice and you can decorate the ice with cut fruit, berries, flowers or floating candles. Alternatively, rest them in a bowl filled with ice and stick in some sparklers!

How about offering a separate or communal dipping bowl with toasted coconut flakes, chopped nuts, or melted chocolate (see opposite). You can also offer individual glasses of alcohol to dip the lollies into, like rum, vodka or prosecco.

The festive season
Layered ice lollies of different fruits, flavours and colours can be made to celebrate occasions, for instance, red white and blue, strawberry, vanilla and blackberry for US Independence Day, or cranberry red for Christmas.

Weddings or romantic evenings
Edible flowers and herbs look beautiful inside a lolly (see page 19).

After dinner
Burgundy Berry or Sweet Sherry & Raisin are good after-dinner delicacies. At the end of a heavy meal, Clementine, White Wine & Rose, Cucumber & Lime, or White Grapefruit & Star Anise are better.

Cocktail parties
Mojito, Ruby Grapefruit & Campari or Drenched Watermelon are good and most fruit-based lollies can be dipped into a cocktail.

Outdoor activities
Lollies are a perfect choice for garden parties, picnics and barbecues (see page 23 for advice on transporting them).

Children
They especially love Milk & Honey, Orange & Lemon, Cherry & Redcurrant, Cereal Milk, Minted Milk, 50s Orange Cheesecake or Chocolate. That's what our Lily Roden likes!

THE PROCEDURE
ESSENTIAL TIPS

1 Fill the moulds
When you pour the mixture into the lolly moulds, leave about 5mm at the top to allow the mixture to expand as it freezes. See also page 18.

2 Insert the sticks
Some moulds have a metal tray that you can insert the sticks through. If so, make sure the sticks go in straight otherwise you'll have a really hard time taking the metal tray off when you are ready to unmould them. We prefer to use this method: leave the moulds uncovered in the freezer for about 1 hour (but be careful not to forget them - we've done it many times!), then insert the sticks and they will remain upright. Alternatively, use the foil trick (see page 18).

3 Freeze
Turn your freezer to the coldest setting. The faster the lolly freezes, the smaller the ice crystals will be, which means it will be creamier. Put your moulds at the back of the freezer where it's coldest. Lollies take 4-8 hours to freeze depending on the ingredients you use. The higher the water-to-sugar ratio the faster your lolly will freeze. Alcohol will slow the process and too much will result in a slushy lolly. There are some expensive instant lolly makers that will freeze a lolly in just 15 minutes, so that's an option if you're really impatient.

4 Unmould

Carefully immerse the moulds in hot water (we use the kitchen sink) for about 10-20 seconds, making sure to dip them right up to just below the top rim, then pull hard on the sticks to yank them out. If they don't come out, they might need a second immersion. If you are using individual moulds, you can run hot water over the outside of the mould and then pull hard on the sticks.

5 Eat or store

Enjoy your ice lollies immediately or store them in sealable freezer bags or waxed paper bags in the freezer. Make sure they are airtight to prevent ice crystals from forming inside and a taste of 'freezer burn'. You can also keep them frozen in their moulds until you are ready to eat them but try not to leave them for too long because they taste much better within a week of making.

6 Transport

Use insulated freezer carrier bags or a Styrofoam-lined box if you ever need to transport ice lollies. The more lollies you transport together, the longer they will stay frozen. For a very long journey you may want to purchase a block of dried ice, which will keep them frozen for many hours.

THE LOLLIES

ORANGE & LEMON

This is one of the simplest and most thirst-quenching
combinations there is and it's bursting with flavour. The taste is
so much better if you choose the freshest sweet-tasting oranges
and squeeze them yourself.

- finely grated zest of 1 orange
- 75g granulated sugar
- 4 tablespoons water
- 600ml freshly squeezed orange juice (from about 6 oranges)
- 80ml freshly squeezed lemon juice (from about 3 lemons)

Put the orange zest, sugar and water in a small saucepan and bring
to a simmer. Simmer until the sugar has dissolved, then stir the
syrup into the orange and lemon juices.

Pour the mixture into your ice-lolly moulds, leaving 5mm at the
top to allow the mixture to expand when it freezes. Insert the lolly
sticks and freeze. (See page 22 for the complete procedure.)

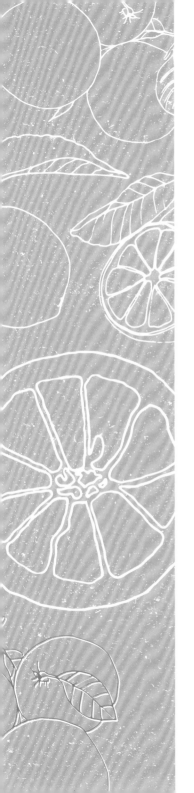

RASPBERRY & LIME

This is sweet and tangy with a subtle undercurrent of lime. We
don't strain out the raspberry seeds for the carts and most people
have no problem with that - in fact they love the realness of it.
But if you prefer a smooth, silky texture we recommend straining
the mixture through a fine sieve.

- 210g granulated sugar
- finely grated zest of 1 lime
- 300ml water
- 500g raspberries, rinsed
- 2-3 tablespoons freshly squeezed lime juice

Put the sugar, lime zest and 100ml of the water in a small saucepan
and bring to a simmer. Simmer until the sugar has dissolved.

Put the raspberries in a food processor with the lime syrup and the
remaining water and blend to a purée. Add 2 tablespoons of the lime
juice and taste to see if it's sharp enough. If not, add a little more
to achieve an equal balance of sweet and sharp.

Pour the mixture into your ice-lolly moulds, leaving 5mm at the
top to allow the mixture to expand when it freezes. Insert the lolly
sticks and freeze. (See page 22 for the complete procedure.)

LEMON & GINGER

This is a favourite choice for those who love contrasting sensations. Prepare for something intense, sweet, spicy – and mouth-puckering.

- 7-cm piece of fresh ginger, peeled and finely chopped or grated
- 800ml water
- 170g granulated sugar
- finely grated zest of 3 lemons
- 75ml freshly squeezed lemon juice (from about 3 lemons)
- 8-10 extra-thin lemon slices (optional)

Put the ginger, water, sugar and lemon zest in a small saucepan and bring to a simmer. Simmer until the sugar has dissolved, then remove the pan from the heat and allow the syrup to cool to room temperature.

Pour the mixture through a fine sieve, pressing down hard on the pieces of ginger with the back of a spoon to extract all the juices. Mix in the lemon juice.

Pour the mixture into your ice-lolly moulds, leaving 5mm at the top to allow the mixture to expand when it freezes. Place a slice of lemon, if using, into each mould, then insert a lolly stick and freeze. (See page 22 for the complete procedure.)

BLACKBERRY

When my daughter Lily and I stay with my mother over the summer, we test the blackberries on the roadside outside her house until they're just sweet enough and then we have fun turning these into dark purple-striped lollies by mixing in a touch of cream or yoghurt. They look like Rothco paintings.

- 500g blackberries
- 130g granulated sugar
- 3 teaspoons freshly squeezed lime or lemon juice
- 400ml water
- 6 tablespoons double cream or Greek yoghurt (optional)

Put the blackberries, sugar, lime or lemon juice and water in a food processor and blend gradually to a purée.

Pour the mixture into a fine sieve, stir it through and press down on the solids with the back of a spoon to extract all the liquid.

If you want to make stripes, divide the blackberry mixture in half. Add the cream to one half and mix it in well. Pour enough pure blackberry mixture into each ice-lolly mould to reach about one-quarter of the way up. (See page 19 for more help on creating stripes.)

Freeze until slightly firm, about 1 hour, then pour the cream mixture on top. Freeze for a further hour, then top with the remaining pure blackberry mixture. Insert a lolly stick when all the layers are in. They should stay upright due to the half-frozen last layers. Freeze completely. (See page 22 for the complete procedure.)

ICE KITCHEN

STRAWBERRIES & CREAM

This English classic is wonderful as it is, but look how it can be transformed with the inspired variations below.

 8-10

- 110g plus 2 tablespoons granulated sugar
- 125ml water
- 450g strawberries, rinsed, hulled and cut in half
- 2 tablespoons freshly squeezed lemon juice
- 40ml double cream

Put the 110g sugar and the water in a small saucepan and bring to a simmer. Simmer until the sugar has dissolved.

Put the strawberries, sugar syrup and lemon juice in a food processor and blend to a purée.

Stir the 2 tablespoons sugar into the cream. Divide the cream between your ice-lolly moulds (about 1 tablespoon cream each), then pour the strawberry mixture on top. Insert the lolly sticks and freeze. (See page 22 for the complete procedure.)

Variations:
Turn this into a French classic by adding 5 tablespoons red wine to the strawberries.

For an Italian spin add 2 tablespoons balsamic vinegar, a pinch of pepper and 2 tablespoons finely chopped fresh basil to the mix.

For an exotic touch, add 1 tablespoon rose water to the cream.
And I like to add 5 tablespoons sweet sherry to the strawberries.

TART PLUM

There are endless varieties of plum and they all work beautifully in a lolly. It's the skins that give the most flavour and that turn a plum into a tart plum when poached. Apparently there are more plum varieties in the world than there are of any other fruit. The promiscuous plum!

- 700g plums, rinsed, quartered and pitted
- 350ml water
- 100-120g granulated sugar (depending on the sweetness of the plums)
- 4 tablespoons freshly squeezed lemon juice
- 4 tablespoons elderflower cordial (optional)
- 1 tablespoon double cream per lolly (optional)

Put the plums, water, sugar and lemon juice in a saucepan and bring to a simmer. Simmer for 10-15 minutes until the plums break down. Remove the pan from the heat and allow the mixture to cool for a few minutes. Transfer the mixture to a food processor and add the elderflower cordial, if using. Blend, making sure you allow some small chunks to remain.

Pour the mixture into your ice-lolly moulds, leaving 5mm at the top to allow the mixture to expand when it freezes. You can create a stripe with 2 different types of plum - see page 19. Insert the lolly sticks and freeze. (See page 22 for the complete procedure.)

Variations:
Greengage plum is one of our favourites and pairs well with elderflower - add 4 tablespoons elderflower cordial. Plums also pair well with almond - add 1 teaspoon almond extract. A tablespoon of freshly grated ginger can also add a nice kick.

ICE KITCHEN

CANTALOUPE & BASIL

Choose a sweetly fragrant Cantaloupe melon that seems heavy for its size. It's great with just lemon or lime in a lolly, but adding fresh basil adds complexity of flavour.

- 170ml water
- 75g granulated sugar
- 15 fresh basil leaves (optional)
- 600g cantaloupe melon chunks (from about 1 small melon)
- 4 tablespoons freshly squeezed lime or lemon juice

Put the water, sugar and basil, if using, in a small saucepan and bring to a simmer. Simmer until the sugar has dissolved.

Remove the pan from the heat and allow the mixture to cool to room temperature. Pick out the basil leaves, squeezing any juice back into the pan.

Put the cantaloupe chunks in a food processor and blend to a smooth purée. Add the basil syrup and lime or lemon juice and blend again.

Pour the mixture into your ice-lolly moulds, leaving 5mm at the top to allow the mixture to expand when it freezes. Insert the lolly sticks and freeze. (See page 22 for the complete procedure.)

Variations:
Try using fresh mint or tarragon instead of basil.

Cantaloupe and honeydew melons pair well with fresh ginger - add 2 tablespoons freshly grated ginger to the syrup.

Melon is also nice with port - add 3-4 tablespoons to the food processor.

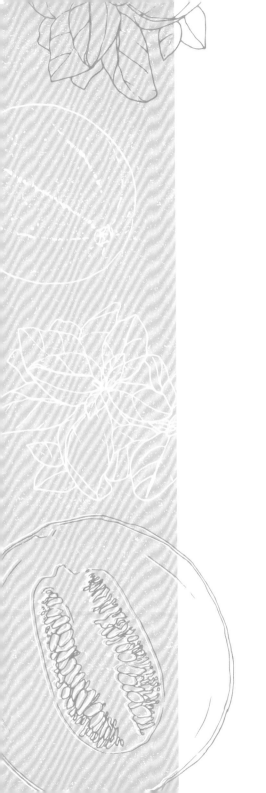

LYCHEE & LEMONGRASS

This recipe requires a little labour but if you love lychees then it becomes a labour of love. It's always better to use fresh fruit but in this case you could also use tinned lychee. This lolly has a very special, delicate and distinctive flavour in which both the lychee and lemongrass shine through.

8-10

- 2 lemongrass stalks
- 350ml water
- 75g granulated sugar
- finely grated zest of 1 lime
- 500g lychees (from about 22-25 lychees), peeled and pitted
- 2-3 tablespoons freshly squeezed lime juice

Slice the lemongrass stalks into 5-mm pieces and put them in a small saucepan with the water, sugar and lime zest. Bring to a simmer and simmer for 3 minutes to extract the lemongrass aroma.

Remove the pan from the heat and allow the syrup to steep for at least 10 minutes. Pour the syrup through a fine sieve, pressing down hard on the pieces of lemongrass and lime zest to extract the juices.

Put the lychee flesh in a food processor and blend until smooth. Add the lemongrass syrup and blend again. Sieve the mixture again, into a bowl, and stir in the lime juice.

Pour the mixture into your ice-lolly moulds, leaving 5mm at the top to allow the mixture to expand when it freezes. Insert the lolly sticks and freeze. (See page 22 for the complete procedure.)

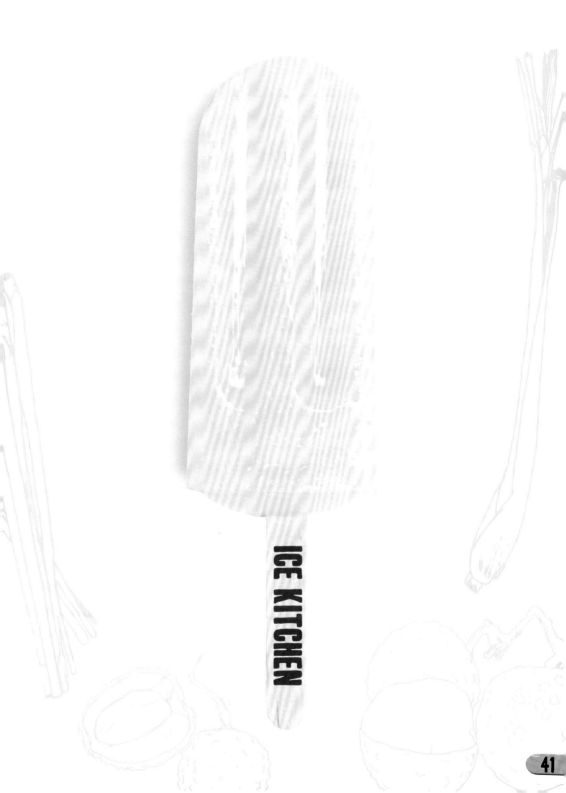

ICE KITCHEN

DRENCHED WATERMELON

● ● ● ● ● ● ● ● ● ● ● ● ● ● ●

If you're wondering why this lolly's called 'drenched', it's because
we suggest squeezing lime juice over it as you eat it. Out of
curiosity one morning, I started dipping this lolly into white rum
- it was so good that I couldn't stop! Try it - just make sure you do
it in the evening rather than the morning...!

- ● 4 tablespoons water
- ● 65g granulated sugar
- ● 700g watermelon flesh, deseeded and cut into chunks
- ● 5 tablespoons freshly squeezed lime juice
- ● a pinch of salt
- ● 2 limes, cut into wedges to squeeze on the lollies as you eat them

Put the water and sugar in a small saucepan and bring to a simmer.
Simmer until the sugar has dissolved.

Remove the pan from the heat and allow the syrup to cool for a few
minutes. Meanwhile, put the watermelon in a food processor and
blend until smooth. Add the lime juice, salt and sugar syrup and
blend again. If there are any seeds, strain the mixture through a
fine sieve.

Pour the mixture into your ice-lolly moulds, leaving 5mm at the
top to allow the mixture to expand when it freezes. Insert the lolly
sticks and freeze. (See page 22 for the complete procedure.)

Squeeze fresh lime juice on the frozen lolly as you eat it and also
dip it in white rum if you like.

Variation:
Throw a handful of torn mint leaves into the sugar syrup as it heats.
When cooled, squeeze the leaves with your fingers before discarding.

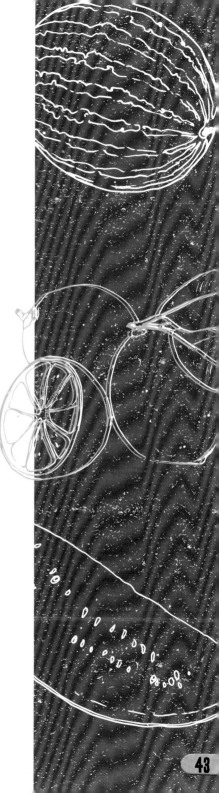

STRAWBERRY & PEPPER

The bite of black pepper in a fruit lolly is very interesting, but wearing a cap of white chocolate is truly inspired. Good going Cesar, and it looks artistic too!

- 50g granulated sugar
- 3 tablespoons water
- 450g strawberries, rinsed, hulled and cut in half
- a squeeze of lemon juice
- 30 black peppercorns, finely ground or smashed

Put the sugar and water in a small saucepan over a medium heat and bring to a simmer. Simmer until the sugar has dissolved.

Put the strawberries in a food processor and blend to a purée. Add the sugar syrup, lemon juice and pepper and blend again.

Pour the mixture into your ice-lolly moulds, leaving 5mm at the top to allow the mixture to expand when it freezes. Insert the lolly sticks and freeze. (See page 22 for the complete procedure.)

This is great on its own, but to give it a white chocolate cap, follow the instructions on page 20.

ICE KITCHEN

PEACHES & CREAM

Choose peaches that are fragrant and firm with a little give;
they are at their best at the height of summer. Poaching them
intensifies their flavour.

- 750g peaches (about 4 large or 8 small peaches)
- 250ml water
- 100g granulated sugar
- freshly squeezed juice of 1 lemon
- 1 teaspoon vanilla extract (optional)
- 75ml double cream

Plunge the peaches in boiling water and leave for 2 minutes. The
skins will come loose, so you should be able to peel them off easily.

Pit the peaches and cut them into chunks. Put the water, sugar and
lemon juice in a wide saucepan and bring to a simmer. Simmer until
the sugar has dissolved, then add the peach chunks. Simmer for a
further 5 minutes, or until the peaches are tender. Remove the pan
from the heat and allow to cool to room temperature.

Put the peaches, syrup and vanilla, if using, in a food processor and
blend to a purée. Mix the cream in, or pour 1 teaspoon cream into
each ice-lolly mould. Pour the mixture into the moulds, leaving 5mm
at the top to allow the mixture to expand when it freezes. Insert
the lolly sticks and freeze. (See page 22 for the complete procedure.)

Variation:
To make peach Bellini lollies, leave out the cream and add 100ml
Prosecco to the mix, or just dip the lolly into Prosecco as you eat it.

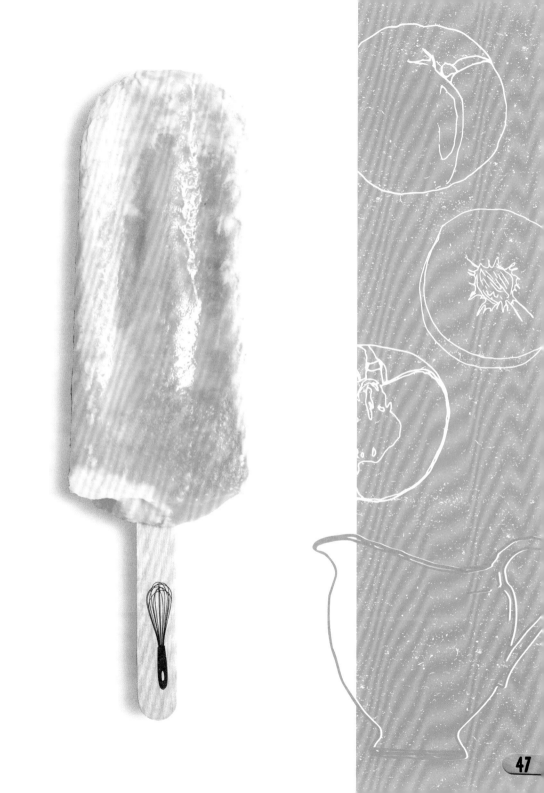

BLUEBERRY & YOGHURT

Now that blueberries are abundant, their popularity has soared. This is great because the health benefits and flavour are utterly delightful, especially when teamed with their old friend yoghurt.

- 300g blueberries
- 75ml plus 2 tablespoons water
- 65g granulated sugar
- 500g Greek yoghurt
- 160g (8 tablespoons) runny honey
- 3 tablespoons freshly squeezed lemon juice

Put the blueberries, 75ml water and sugar in a saucepan and bring to a simmer. Simmer over a low heat for 3-5 minutes until the blueberries burst. Remove the pan from the heat and set aside.

Mix together the yoghurt, honey, lemon juice and the 2 tablespoons water in a bowl.

Spoon alternate layers of the yoghurt and blueberry mixtures into each ice-lolly mould, leaving 5mm at the top to allow the mixture to expand when it freezes. Insert the lolly sticks and freeze. (See page 22 for the complete procedure.)

APRICOT & PISTACHIO

Apricots make deliciously velvety lollies. Make them in mid summer before the apricots vanish for the year again. Choose ones that are only very slightly soft and have a sweet aroma, as those are the tastiest. This combination has a Middle Eastern charm.

- 375ml water
- 130g granulated sugar
- 2 tablespoons freshly squeezed lemon juice
- 500g apricots, cut in half and pitted
- ½ teaspoon almond extract
- 35g shelled pistachios, chopped

Put the water, sugar and lemon juice in a medium saucepan and bring to a simmer. Simmer until the sugar has dissolved.

Add the apricots and simmer until they have broken down – about 5-10 minutes. Remove the pan from the heat and allow the mixture to cool to room temperature.

Stir in the almond extract and chopped pistachios until well mixed.

Pour the mixture into your ice-lolly moulds, leaving 5mm at the top to allow the mixture to expand when it freezes. Insert the lolly sticks and freeze. (See page 22 for the complete procedure.)

It's nice to roll the lollies in pistachios before serving, too (see page 20).

Variation:
You can add 175ml double cream to the apricots after they're cooked, and only use 200ml water.

PEACH & TARRAGON

Cesar likes to roast the peaches for these lollies, as this gives them a slightly caramelised quality. There's no need to peel the peaches as their skins add to the texture and depth here. This recipe will also work for nectarines, apricots or plums.

- 200ml water
- 100g granulated sugar
- leaves from 6 fresh leafy tarragon sprigs
- 750g peaches (about 4 large or 8 small peaches), cut in half
- 2 tablespoons freshly squeezed lemon juice
- 2 teaspoons vanilla extract

Preheat the oven to 180°C/350°F.

Put the water, sugar and tarragon leaves in a small saucepan and bring to a simmer. Simmer until the sugar has dissolved. Remove the pan from the heat and allow the mixture to cool while you roast the peaches.

Place the peaches on a baking tray. Bake them in the preheated oven for about 30 minutes until they are tender. Take them out of the oven and set them aside until they are cool enough to handle.

Pit the peaches and put the flesh, tarragon syrup, lemon juice and vanilla in a food processor. Blend to a purée.

Pour the mixture into your ice-lolly moulds, leaving 5mm at the top to allow the mixture to expand when it freezes. Insert the lolly sticks and freeze. (See page 22 for the complete procedure.)

RUBY GRAPEFRUIT & CAMPARI

This was the first lolly we ever made. It became a signature flavour along the High Line in New York and has remained a favourite in London at the South Bank.

- 125ml water
- 110g granulated sugar
- 600ml fresh ruby red grapefruit juice (from about 4 grapefruits)
- 75ml Campari

Put the water and sugar in a small saucepan and bring to a simmer. Simmer until the sugar has dissolved. Mix together with the grapefruit juice and Campari.

Pour the mixture into your ice-lolly moulds, leaving 5mm at the top to allow the mixture to expand when it freezes. Insert the lolly sticks and freeze. (See page 22 for the complete procedure.)

SWEET PEAR & GINGER

Pear and ginger are a classic pairing. You can use any variety here, like Bosc, Comice, Williams, Anjou or Forelle, and we often use Comice. For extra indulgence, try melting a little dark chocolate and drizzling it into the pear mixture.

8-10

- 200ml water
- 100–120g granulated sugar (depending on the sweetness of the pears)
- 7-cm piece of fresh ginger, peeled and finely chopped or grated
- 875g pears (3-4 pears)
- 3 tablespoons freshly squeezed lemon juice
- 150ml double cream or crème fraîche (optional)

Put the water, sugar and ginger in a wide saucepan and bring to a simmer. Simmer for 3 minutes, then remove the pan from the heat and allow the syrup to cool for a few minutes.

Pour the syrup through a fine sieve, pressing down hard on the pieces of ginger with the back of a spoon to extract all the juices. We leave some ginger pieces in for a stronger ginger taste.

Peel, core and chop the pears, then put them immediately in the syrup so that they don't turn brown. Cover the pan and simmer until tender – about 10 minutes. Remove the pan from the heat and add the lemon juice. Allow the pears and syrup to cool for a few minutes. Put the cooled pears and syrup in a food processor and lightly blend to a purée. Stir in the cream or crème fraîche, if using.

Pour the mixture into your ice-lolly moulds, leaving 5mm at the top to allow the mixture to expand when it freezes. Insert the lolly sticks and freeze. (See page 22 for the complete procedure.)

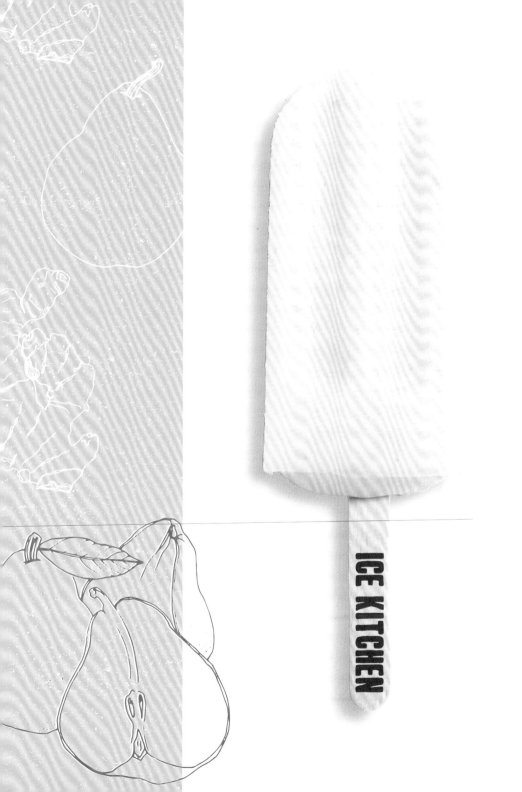

ICE KITCHEN

CHERRY & REDCURRANT

The characteristics of cherry and redcurrant combine for a sweet and tart treat in this pretty lolly. It requires a little patience to create the stripes, but it's fun for kids and for the child at heart.

For the cherry stripe:
- 400ml water
- 120-140g granulated sugar
- 500g cherries
- 4 tablespoons freshly squeezed lemon juice
- ¼ teaspoon almond extract (optional)

For the redcurrant stripe:
- 150g redcurrants
- 300ml water
- 60g granulated sugar

For the cherry stripe, put the water and sugar in a saucepan and bring to a simmer. Simmer until the sugar has dissolved. Add the cherries and simmer for 20 minutes, covered with a lid. Pour the cherries and syrup through a fine sieve, stirring hard and pressing down on the cherries with the back of a spoon to extract all the juices. Discard the cherry pits and skins. Stir in the lemon juice and almond extract, if using.

For the redcurrant stripe, put the redcurrants, water and sugar in a saucepan and bring to a simmer. Simmer for 5 minutes, or until the currants burst. Put the mixture in a food processor and blend to a purée. Strain through a fine sieve, stirring well and pressing down hard on the solids with the back of a spoon to extract all the juices.

To create the stripes, freeze alternate layers of cherry and redcurrant in your ice-lolly moulds. Freeze each layer for about 1 hour, leaving 5mm at the top of the mould after the last layer to allow the mixture to expand when it freezes. Insert the lolly sticks when all the layers are in. They should stay upright due to the half-frozen last layers. Freeze completely. (See page 22 for the complete procedure.)

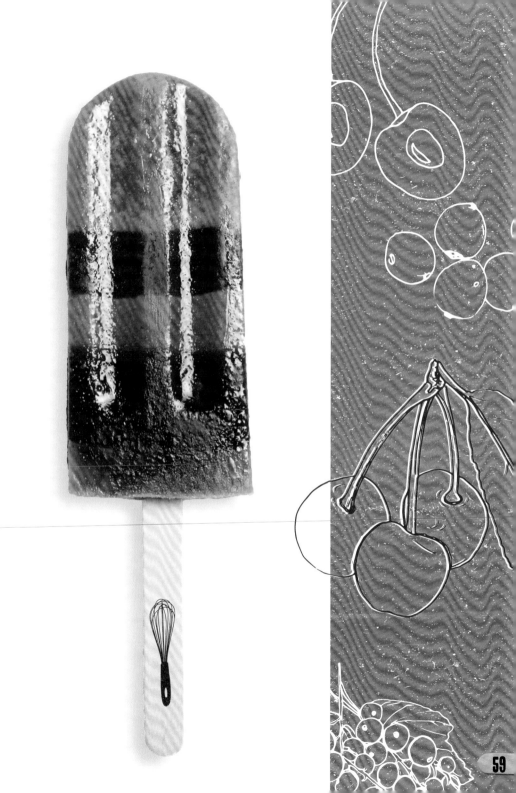

FRESH MANGO

Cesar dedicates this to Meekal, one of his favourite customers down at the South Bank market. He often bought 2 lollies for each of his 3 kids and we had to promise him we'd hold reserves over the winter. The key to this recipe is finding the juiciest, ripest and most flavourful mangoes. There are so many Pakistani and Indian varieties, each with their own sweet, unique character. We love Pakistani honey mangoes, and Indian Alphonso and Kesar mangoes.

- 4-5 medium Indian or Pakistani mangoes, or 3-4 larger Brazilian or other mangoes
- a squeeze of lemon juice
- 250ml water

Peel the mangoes and carefully cut the flesh away from the central pit, facing the knife away from yourself.

Put the mango flesh in a processor and blend - you should get about 500ml smooth mango pulp.

Add a tiny squeeze of lemon juice. You should barely be able to taste the lemon at this point - it should just lift the amazing mango flavour. Add the water and blend again.

Pour the mixture into your ice-lolly moulds, leaving 5mm at the top to allow the mixture to expand when it freezes. Insert the lolly sticks and freeze. (See page 22 for the complete procedure.)

Make sure you make enough to last until next year!

CLEMENTINE, WHITE WINE & ROSE

A man in a Spanish wine shop suggested this combination from a drink he remembered and it turned out beautifully. Make this light, elegant lolly using the Spanish white wine Verdejo - zesty, with tropical notes - or substitute another dry white wine. The optional basil leaves add a complexity to the flavour.

8–10

- finely grated zest of 2 clementines
- 5 tablespoons water
- 110g granulated sugar
- small handful of fresh basil leaves (optional)
- 125ml white wine (Verdejo is best)
- 500ml freshly squeezed clementine juice (from about 12 clementines)
- 3 tablespoons freshly squeezed lemon juice
- 1 tablespoon rose water

Put the clementine zest, water, sugar and basil leaves, if using, in a small saucepan and bring to a simmer. Simmer until the sugar has dissolved. Remove the pan from the heat and allow the mixture to cool to room temperature.

Pick out the basil leaves, squeezing any juice back into the pan. Pour the wine, clementine and lemon juices, and rose water into the sugar syrup and mix well.

Pour the mixture into your ice-lolly moulds, leaving 5mm at the top to allow the mixture to expand when it freezes. Insert the lolly sticks and freeze. (See page 22 for the complete procedure.)

PINEAPPLE & COCONUT

This child-friendly combination is an escape to the sun. We love the sweet acidity of the pineapple with the mellow coconut. Adults can dip this in rum or sprinkle coconut flakes on top, or they can add rum to the mixture to turn it into a Piña Colada. Choose a plump pineapple with a sweet scent and healthy green leaves.

- 1 pineapple
- freshly squeezed juice and finely grated zest of 1 lemon
- 130g granulated sugar
- 400ml unsweetened coconut milk
- 4 tablespoons rum (optional)

Cut the crown off the pineapple and discard. Cut the pineapple in half lengthways, cut away the peel with a sharp knife and cut out any remaining 'eyes'. Cut each half in half again, lengthways. Cut away and discard the hard core, then cube the flesh.

Put the pineapple cubes, lemon juice and zest, sugar and coconut milk in a food processor and blend, allowing some chunks to remain. Taste and add more sugar, if needed. If you decide to add rum, stir it in now.

Pour the mixture into your ice-lolly moulds, leaving 5mm at the top to allow the mixture to expand when it freezes. Insert the lolly sticks and freeze. (See page 22 for the complete procedure.)

Variation:
For a sharper, very lively-tasting lolly, replace the coconut milk with 375ml fresh orange juice or water and dip the frozen lolly in coconut flakes, if you like.

ICE KITCHEN

COCONUT & LIME

You know the song – now here's the lolly! (If you don't know the Harry Nilsson song, 'Coconut' in which he sings about putting the lime in the coconut, then go have a listen and enjoy yourself!) The lolly is tangy, creamy and so easy to make, and it really benefits from being made with good-quality coconut milk.

- 400ml unsweetened coconut milk
- finely grated zest of 2 limes
- 150ml freshly squeezed lime juice (from about 4-5 limes)
- 400g sweetened condensed milk
- a good pinch of salt

Put all the ingredients into a large bowl and mix with a spoon until fully blended.

Pour the mixture into your ice-lolly moulds, leaving 5mm at the top to allow the mixture to expand when it freezes. Insert the lolly sticks and freeze. (See page 22 for the complete procedure.)

When ready to eat, it's nice to dip the lolly in toasted desiccated coconut. Or splash it with rum!

BANANA CHOCODIP

Monkey around with this lolly that children love. You can add
a couple of spoons of Nutella, peanut butter or oat bran to the
mix if you desire – it's all good! The banana flavour mysteriously
intensifies the longer the lollies stay frozen.

- 3 medium bananas
- 1 teaspoon freshly squeezed lemon juice
- 150ml double cream
- 175ml whole milk
- ½ teaspoon vanilla extract
- 4 tablespoons maple syrup or honey
- 100g milk or dark chocolate
- 1 tablespoon vegetable oil

Put the bananas, lemon juice, cream, milk, vanilla, and maple syrup
or honey in a food processor and blend until smooth.

Pour the mixture into your ice-lolly moulds, leaving 5mm at the
top to allow the mixture to expand when it freezes. Insert the lolly
sticks and freeze. (See page 22 for the complete procedure.)

To cap the frozen lollies with chocolate, see page 20.

ICE KITCHEN

CRANBERRY & ORANGE

This is the perfect way to end a rich Christmas dinner: deck the halls with this festive lolly! If you're sitting around the table, try dipping the lolly into a bowl of orange liqueur or vodka.

- 500ml water
- 160g plus 2 tablespoons granulated sugar
- 200g cranberries
- 200ml freshly squeezed orange juice (from about 2 oranges)
- freshly squeezed juice of 1 lemon
- 100ml double cream or crème fraîche

Put the water and the 160g sugar in a medium saucepan and bring to a simmer. Simmer until the sugar has dissolved. Drop in the cranberries and simmer for a further 6 minutes or until the berries have burst and the juices are released.

Remove the pan from the heat and allow to cool to room temperature.

Put the mixture in a food processor and blend to a purée. Pour the mixture through a fine sieve, pressing with the back of a spoon to extract all the juices. Stir in the orange and lemon juices.

Stir the 2 tablespoons sugar into the cream. Divide the cranberry mixture in half and stir the cream into one half. Mix lightly. Divide the cranberry cream between your ice-lolly moulds. (See page 19 for more help on creating stripes.)

Freeze until slightly firm, about 1 hour, then pour the pure cranberry mixture on top. Insert the lolly sticks and freeze completely. (See page 22 for the complete procedure.)

RHUBARB & CUSTARD

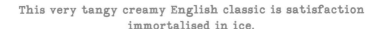

This very tangy creamy English classic is satisfaction
immortalised in ice.

For the rhubarb:
- 300ml water
- 110g granulated sugar
- 400g rhubarb, trimmed and roughly chopped

For the custard:
- 400ml whole milk
- 200ml double cream
- 4 egg yolks
- 120g granulated sugar
- 2 teaspoons vanilla extract
- a pinch of salt

For the rhubarb, put the water and sugar in a medium saucepan and bring to a simmer. Simmer until the sugar has dissolved. Add the rhubarb and simmer for a further 10 minutes, or until the rhubarb has broken down. Remove the pan from the heat.

For the custard, pour the milk and cream in a saucepan over a low heat. Beat the egg yolks and sugar together in a heatproof bowl. When the milk starts to simmer, take it off the heat and spoon a few ladles of it into the egg mixture. Whisk it well, then pour it back into the pan. Heat up the mixture again over a low-medium heat, stirring constantly, until it has thickened enough to easily coat the back of a wooden spoon. Do not let it boil. Pour it immediately into a bowl, stir in the vanilla and salt and allow it to cool down before refrigerating it for a couple of hours or overnight to thicken.

Spoon alternate layers of rhubarb and custard into your ice-lolly moulds, leaving 5mm at the top to allow the mixture to expand when it freezes. Insert the lolly sticks and freeze. (See page 22 for the complete procedure.)

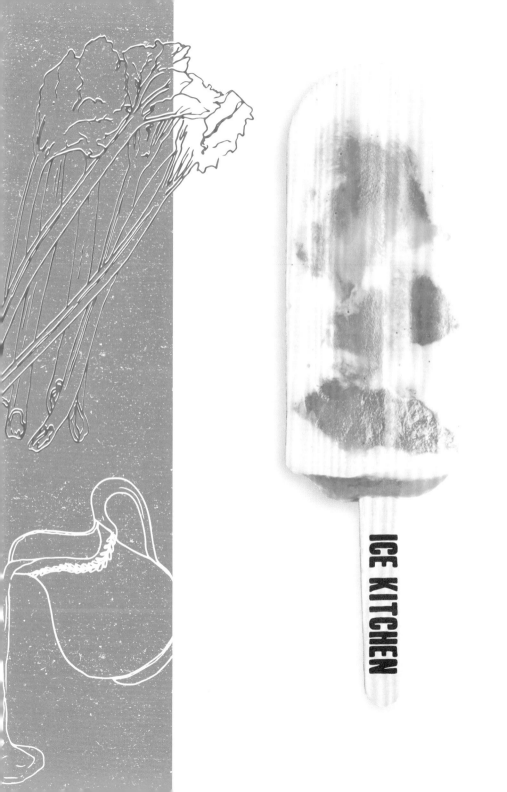

ICE KITCHEN

WHITE GRAPEFRUIT & STAR ANISE

Star anise is the fruit of a 25-foot Chinese evergreen magnolia tree. Its subtle liquorice aroma shines through the sharpness of the grapefruit. Make sure you use the yellow-skinned (called 'white') grapefruit variety and steep the star anise for as long as possible in the sugar syrup. We steep it overnight. For an extra spike, you can dip this lolly in a glass of anise-flavoured liqueur, such as Pernod, Pastis, ouzo or arak. It makes an exciting pre-dinner treat.

- 125ml water
- 120g granulated sugar
- grated zest of 1 white grapefruit
- 4-6 whole star anise
- 600ml freshly squeezed white grapefruit juice
  (from about 4-5 grapefruits)

Put the water, sugar, grapefruit zest and star anise in a saucepan and bring to a simmer. Simmer for 5 minutes. Remove the pan from the heat and allow the star anise to infuse at least until the syrup has cooled to room temperature, but preferably overnight.

Pull out the star anise from the mixture, but it does look beautiful if you then drop one inside the ice-lolly mould before filling. Add the grapefruit juice to the syrup and stir. Pour the mixture into your ice-lolly moulds, leaving 5mm at the top to allow the mixture to expand when it freezes. Insert the lolly sticks and freeze. (See page 22 for the complete procedure.)

EGYPTIAN HIBISCUS & PEACH

The ancient Egyptian hibiscus drink called 'karkadé' inspired this sweet and tart, ruby-coloured lolly. It is very popular in Egypt where our family came from and in the Sudan where my grandparents and Cesar's great grandparents once lived. You can find dried hibiscus in most Middle Eastern shops.

- 40g dried hibiscus, briefly rinsed in cold water
- 850ml water
- 125g plus 2 tablespoons granulated sugar
- 2 peaches, pitted and cut into slim wedges

Put the hibiscus and water in a medium saucepan, bring to the boil and simmer for 5 minutes. Remove the pan from the heat and stir in the 125g sugar. Allow the mixture to steep for a few hours.

Strain the mixture through a fine sieve, pressing on the hibiscus with the back of a spoon to extract the liquid, or squeeze it with your hands. Put the peaches in a small bowl, sprinkle with the 2 tablespoons of sugar and allow them to macerate for 30 minutes. Put a few macerated peach slices and their juices into each ice-lolly mould, then pour the hibiscus mixture in, leaving 5mm at the top to allow the mixture to expand when it freezes. Insert the lolly sticks and freeze. (See page 22 for the complete procedure.)

Variations:
Mix 1 teaspoon orange blossom or rose water, or 1 teaspoon freshly grated ginger into the hibiscus water after you take it off the heat, or mix it into the peaches.

BURGUNDY BERRY

This mix of berries and wine is great to serve after dinner or at a garden party. Careful not to let your hand slip, as too much alcohol will result in a slushy lolly. Pour a little cream at the bottom of each mould for something extra sublime.

- 250g fresh berries, e.g. raspberries, blackberries, blueberries, plus 170g blackberries
- 140g granulated sugar
- 2 teaspoons freshly squeezed lemon juice
- 125ml Burgundy (or red wine of your choice)
- 125ml water
- 100ml double cream (optional)

Put the 250g fresh berries in a bowl, stir in 80g of the sugar, and the lemon juice and set aside to macerate for at least 1 hour until the juices are released.

Meanwhile, put the wine, water, the 170g blackberries and remaining sugar in a food processor and gently blend. Pour the mixture through a fine sieve, stirring with a spoon and pressing down to extract all the juices.

If using the cream, drizzle a teaspoon into each ice-lolly mould, then loosely press the macerated berries into each mould and pour the wine mixture over them, leaving 5mm at the top to allow the mixture to expand when it freezes. Insert the lolly sticks and freeze. (See page 22 for the complete procedure.)

MOJITO

We created this lolly for an outdoor summer wedding party near London. It's Cesar's favourite cocktail and we were determined to develop it as a lolly. It's since become a top-seller at the cart on the South Bank for people to wind down with in the evening along the river. If you put too much rum in this it will turn mushy, so if you want more, dip the frozen lolly in rum as you eat it.

8-10

- 500ml water
- 155g granulated sugar
- 20g fresh mint leaves plus 20 extra leaves
- 200ml freshly squeezed lime juice (from about 5-6 limes)
- 4 tablespoons white rum
- 10 extra thin lime slices to suspend in the moulds

Put the water and sugar in a small saucepan and bring to the boil. Remove the pan from the heat and drop in the 20g of mint leaves. Cover with a lid, refrigerate and steep for a few hours or overnight.

Strain the syrup through a fine sieve, squeezing any juice from the mint leaves back into the pan. Finely chop 10 of the 20 extra mint leaves and add them to the syrup with the lime juice and rum and mix well. It should taste quite sharp.

Drop a slice of lime into each ice-lolly mould along with a mint leaf. Ladle in the mixture, leaving 5mm at the top to allow the mixture to expand when it freezes. Insert the lolly sticks (the lime slices will be pushed down again to the bottom by the sticks) and freeze. (See page 22 for the complete procedure.)

ICE KITCHEN

SWEET SHERRY & RAISIN

This treasure of a lolly is so good – please try it! I made it for my mother's Spanish book launch party, as it's inspired by the famous Malaga ice cream. The poet laureate Mark Strand was there and said it was the best dessert he'd ever tasted – poetry to my ears!

8-10

- 40g small black raisins or currants
- 60ml Pedro Ximénez (as thick, dark and aged as you can find)
- 350ml double cream
- 250ml whole milk
- 50g granulated sugar
- 1 small cinnamon stick
- 5 egg yolks
- 1 teaspoon vanilla extract

Put the raisins or currants and sherry in a bowl and allow to soak. Put the cream, milk, sugar and cinnamon stick in a small saucepan and heat until almost boiling. Remove the pan from the heat.

In a medium bowl, briefly whisk the egg yolks, then gradually add a ladleful of the hot milk, then another, whisking constantly. Pour this back into the pan. Heat up the mixture again over a low heat, stirring constantly, until it has thickened enough to easily coat the back of a wooden spoon. Do not let it boil. Strain it immediately through a fine sieve into a bowl, stir in the vanilla and allow it to cool before refrigerating it for 2 hours or overnight to thicken.

Add the raisin and sherry mixture to the cold custard and stir gently. Pour the mixture into your ice-lolly moulds, leaving 5mm at the top to allow the mixture to expand when it freezes. Insert the lolly sticks and freeze. (See page 22 for the complete procedure.) If you like, sprinkle on a small pinch of cinnamon on the frozen lolly.

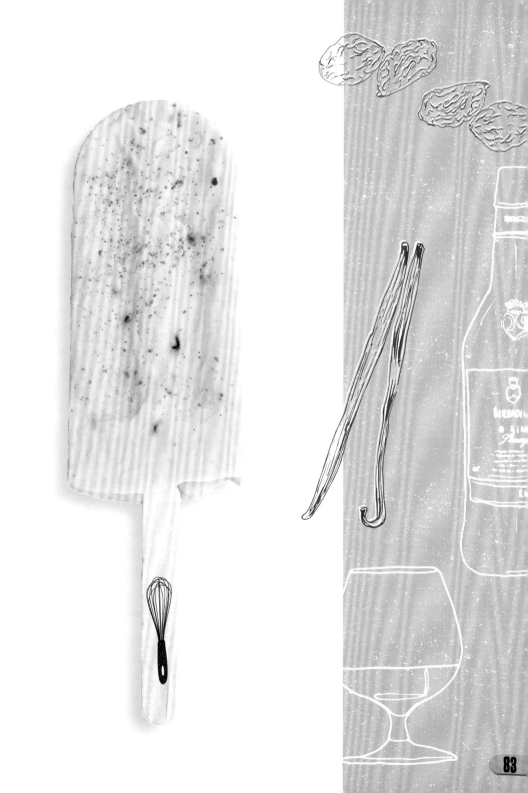

ALMOND &
ORANGE BLOSSOM

There's nothing like the wonderful, delicate taste of almonds and orange blossom together. For me, they conjure up childhood family memories of Middle Eastern pastries. The ground almonds give a very nice texture to this lolly.

- 500ml whole milk
- 20g cornflour
- 250ml double cream
- 125g granulated sugar
- 3 teaspoons orange blossom water
- 5 drops of almond extract
- 40g ground almonds
- handful of flaked almonds, to coat the lollies

Put 3 tablespoons of the milk in a small bowl and mix in the cornflour to form a smooth paste. Pour the remaining milk, the cream and sugar in a medium saucepan and heat until just about to simmer, then stir in the cornflour paste. Stir constantly until the mixture starts to thicken and bubble. Allow to thicken, stirring constantly, for a further 2 minutes.

Pour the mixture through a fine sieve into a bowl. Stir in the orange blossom and almond extract and allow to cool to room temperature.

Stir the ground almonds into the mixture until well blended. Pour the mixture into your ice-lolly moulds, leaving 5mm at the top to allow the mixture to expand when it freezes. Insert the lolly sticks and freeze. (See page 22 for the complete procedure.) When you are ready to enjoy the lollies, roll them in flaked almonds (see page 20).

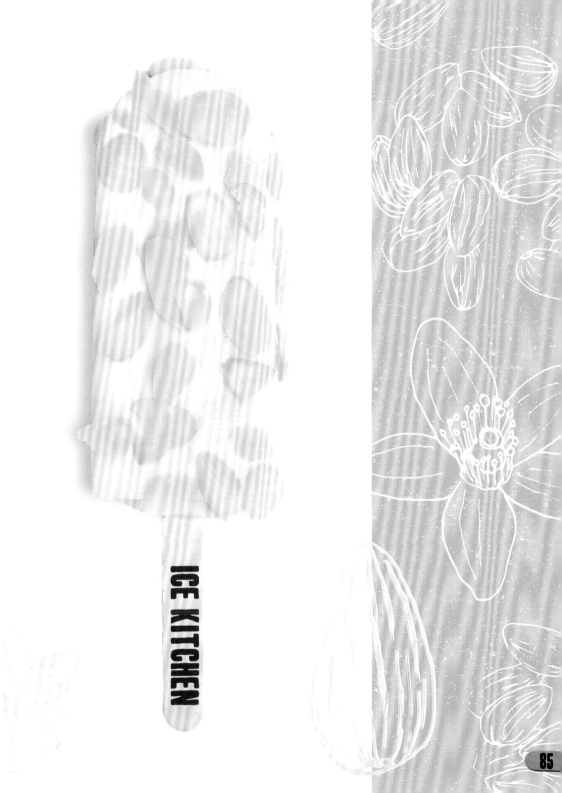

ICE KITCHEN

PISTACHIO & ROSE

I loved the Egyptian milk pudding called 'muhallabeya' that my
mother used to make for me as a child. She sprinkled it with
pistachios and scented it with rose water. Several years ago when
she came to visit me, she helped me to recreate it in this lolly.

- 500ml whole milk
- 25g cornflour
- 250ml double cream
- 125g granulated sugar
- 3 teaspoons rose water (rose waters vary in strength,
  so adjust to taste)
- 40g shelled pistachios, finely chopped

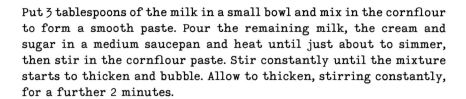

Put 3 tablespoons of the milk in a small bowl and mix in the cornflour
to form a smooth paste. Pour the remaining milk, the cream and
sugar in a medium saucepan and heat until just about to simmer,
then stir in the cornflour paste. Stir constantly until the mixture
starts to thicken and bubble. Allow to thicken, stirring constantly,
for a further 2 minutes.

Pour the mixture through a fine sieve into a bowl. Stir in the rose
water and allow to cool to room temperature.

Stir the pistachios into the mixture until well blended, reserving
a few for coating the lollies. Pour the mixture into your ice-lolly
moulds, leaving 5mm at the top to allow the mixture to expand when
it freezes. Insert the lolly sticks and freeze. (See page 22 for the
complete procedure.)

When you are ready to enjoy the lollies, roll them in more chopped
pistachios (see page 20).

MINTED MILK

We had so many recipes in mind for this book but after composing this one we knew immediately it had to be put in. It's so addictive that Lily devoured every last one in the batch.

- 30g fresh mint leaves (a large bunch of about 20 sprigs)
- 450ml whole milk
- 250ml double cream
- 125g granulated sugar

Crush the mint leaves a little with the back of a spoon: this will help to turn the milk pastel green.

Put the milk, cream and sugar in a saucepan and bring almost to the boil. Remove the pan from the heat and add the mint leaves. Cover and allow to cool. The longer you can let the mint infuse the better. Strain the mixture through a fine sieve, pressing down on the leaves with the back of a spoon or squeezing them with your hands to extract the juices.

Pour the mixture into your ice-lolly moulds, leaving 5mm at the top to allow the mixture to expand when it freezes. Insert the lolly sticks and freeze. (See page 22 for the complete procedure.) If you like you can artfully drip some melted dark chocolate over the lolly (see page 20 for help with melting chocolate).

Variation:
Turn this into a minted chocolate lolly by warming the minted milk up again after you take out the mint leaves, then stirring in 60g chopped dark chocolate. Allow the mixture to cool completely so that the chocolate is fully integrated.

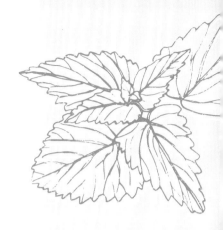

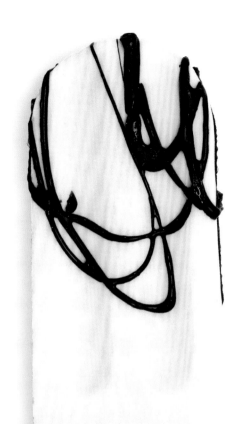

ICE KITCHEN

THREE MILKS LEMON PUDDING

The famous Mexican 'tres leches' cake, made with 3 kinds of milk or cream, is one of the best desserts ever invented. Here we've given it a spin for all lemon lovers. This one's easy!

- 396g sweetened condensed milk
- 150ml whole milk
- 150ml double cream
- 250ml freshly squeezed lemon juice (from about 3 lemons)
- finely grated zest of 2 lemons

Put all the ingredients together in a bowl and whisk until smooth and combined.

Pour the mixture into your ice-lolly moulds, leaving 5mm at the top to allow the mixture to expand when it freezes. Insert the lolly sticks and freeze. (See page 22 for the complete procedure.)

Variation:
If you like, you can crumble some pieces of cake or ladyfingers into the mix.

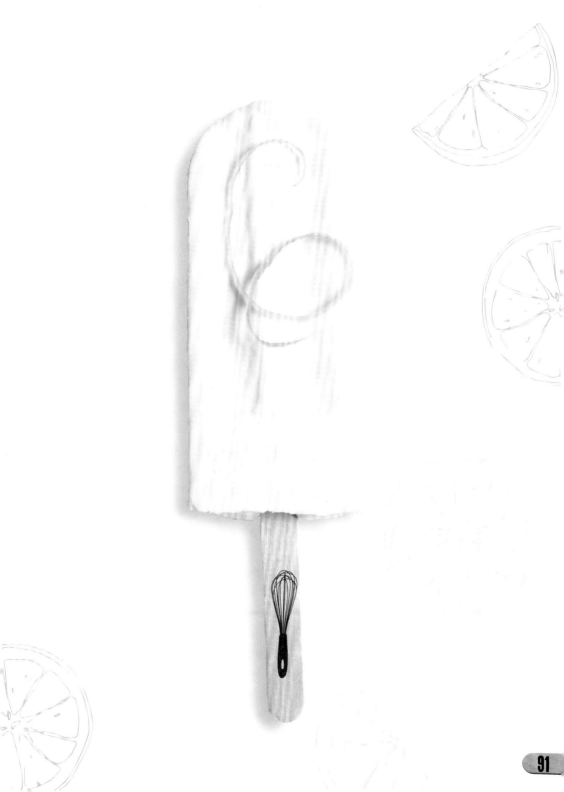

FRENCH TWIST

The marriage of French vanilla and raspberries works so well, which explains why this lolly is so popular at the cart. The small amount of vodka keeps the raspberries from freezing solid.

For the raspberries:
- 300g raspberries (fresh or frozen)
- 100g granulated sugar
- 2 tablespoons vodka (optional)

For the French vanilla:
- 400ml whole milk
- 200ml double cream
- a pinch of salt
- 1 vanilla pod
- 4 egg yolks
- 120g granulated sugar

For the raspberries, put the raspberries in a bowl and pour the sugar and vodka over them. Set aside for at least 1 hour or overnight so the raspberries release their juices.

For the French vanilla, put the milk, cream and salt in a saucepan over a low heat. Cut along the vanilla pod and scrape the seeds out into the pan and add the pod too. Beat the egg yolks and sugar in a heatproof bowl. When the milk starts to simmer, take it off the heat and pour a few spoons of it into the egg mixture. Whisk well, then pour back into the pan. Heat over a low-medium heat, stirring constantly, until thickened enough to easily coat the back of a wooden spoon. Do not let it boil. Strain it immediately through a fine sieve and allow to cool, then refrigerate for at least 2 hours.

Mash the raspberry mixture lightly, leaving some raspberries almost whole. Spoon alternate layers of the raspberries and French vanilla into your ice-lolly moulds, leaving 5mm at the top to allow the mixture to expand when it freezes. Muddle the layers together a little with a lolly stick. Insert the lolly sticks and freeze. (See page 22 for the complete procedure.)

ICE KITCHEN

50s ORANGE CHEESECAKE

Here is a twist on our amazingly popular 50s orange lolly, a real hit with New Yorkers. We've morphed it into a cheesecake! The orange oils from the zest are what gives this a special flavour. It's easy to make and uniquely delicious.

8-10

- finely grated zest of 3 oranges
- 150g granulated sugar
- 90g cream cheese
- 250ml sour cream
- 375ml freshly squeezed orange juice (from about 4 oranges)
- 65g digestive biscuits (optional)

Put the orange zest and sugar in a food processor and whizz for about 1 minute until the sugar is bright orange. Add the cream cheese and blend for a few more seconds. Add the sour cream and blend for another few seconds. Add the orange juice and blend again until fully combined.

Pour the mixture into your ice-lolly moulds, leaving 5mm at the top to allow the mixture to expand when it freezes. Insert the lolly sticks and freeze. (See page 22 for the complete procedure.)

If you like, grind the digestives up with a mortar and pestle and sprinkle on the frozen lollies, or leave the lollies to melt only slightly and lightly dip them in a bowl of crumbs just before eating.

MILK & HONEY

This is what a lolly should be: simple and delicious. The taste of the honey really shines through when it's frozen with milk and cream and it all melts beautifully together as you eat it. It's interesting to experiment with different honeys, such as acacia, orange blossom, lavender or wild flower, or the honeys produced by London's busy bees.

- 160g (8 tablespoons) honey
- 350ml whole milk
- 350ml double cream

Put the honey and 6 tablespoons of the milk in a small saucepan and heat until melted and well blended. Remove the pan from the heat and pour the mixture into a bowl with the cream and remaining milk, stirring until well blended.

Pour the mixture into your ice-lolly moulds, leaving 5mm at the top to allow the mixture to expand when it freezes. Insert the lolly sticks and freeze. (See page 22 for the complete procedure.)

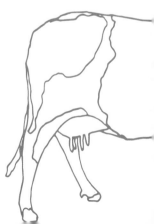

ICE KITCHEN

CASSATA

We've managed to put Italy on a stick here, with this traditional
Sicilian dessert converted to a lolly. Creamy ricotta is mixed with
chopped nuts like almonds and pistachios, chopped candied fruits
and tiny pieces of chocolate.

- 450g ricotta
- 400ml double cream
- 140g caster sugar
- 2½ teaspoons vanilla extract
- 4-6 tablespoons milk, depending on the thickness
  of the ricotta
- 30g candied orange peel
- 30g candied lemon peel
- 30g shelled pistachios
- 30g blanched almonds
- 45g dark chocolate
- 1 teaspoon grated orange or lemon zest (optional)

Put the ricotta, cream, sugar and vanilla in a food processor and
blend very briefly until smooth. (The mix will thicken slightly.)
Pour into a bowl and stir in the milk to thin the mixture, but not
too much as the chopped ingredients need to float in the mixture.

Chop the candied peels, nuts and chocolate into small pieces and stir
into the ricotta mixture. Mix in the zest, if using.

Spoon the mixture into your ice-lolly moulds, and bang the moulds
hard on the table so there are no big air bubbles. Leave 5mm at the
top to allow the mixture to expand when it freezes. Insert the lolly
sticks and freeze. (See page 22 for the complete procedure.) If you
like, save a little chopped chocolate or candied fruit to sprinkle
onto the frozen lollies.

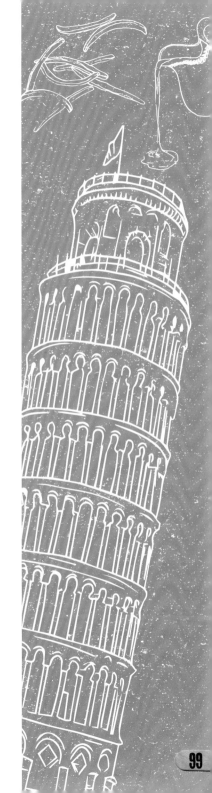

BUTTERSCOTCH

Smooth, silky and comforting, butterscotch is irresistible to both children and adults.

- 100g granulated sugar
- 2 tablespoons unsalted butter
- 250ml double cream
- 625ml whole milk
- 1 teaspoon vanilla extract
- ¼ teaspoon salt

Put the sugar, butter and cream in a saucepan and bring to a simmer over a low heat. Simmer for about 10-12 minutes, stirring occasionally. Keep an eye on it and stir particularly towards the end as the mixture darkens to a dark amber and thickens: this is when the lovely butterscotch flavour develops.

Once it has turned dark amber, stir in the milk and bring back up to a simmer, then simmer for 2 minutes. Remove the pan from the heat, stir in the vanilla and salt and allow to cool to room temperature.

Pour the mixture into your ice-lolly moulds, leaving 5mm at the top to allow the mixture to expand when it freezes. Insert the lolly sticks and freeze. (See page 22 for the complete procedure.)

Variation:
Bourbon is a good match with butterscotch. If you like, add 2-3 tablespoons to the mix at the end.

ICE KITCHEN

SONI'S KULFI

Our friend, Soni Bhatia, a talented chef who trained in Paris and ran the renowned Soni's supper club in San Francisco insisted that we include a kulfi (Indian ice cream) lolly in this book. This is her family recipe and together, we reconstructed it as a lolly. The ground almonds give it a bite, but beware: these lollies are very rich and filled with goodness, so we suggest using smallish moulds.

8-10

- 1.25 litres whole milk
- 2 pinches of saffron threads
- 8 cardamom pods, crushed with a pestle and mortar
- 110g granulated sugar
- 300ml double cream
- 60g ground almonds
- 4-5 drops of kewra essence (optional)
- 35g shelled pistachios, chopped

Put the milk, saffron and cardamom in a wide, heavy saucepan and bring to a boil. Leave a metal whisk in the saucepan to prevent the milk from boiling over. Simmer, and stir every 5 minutes or so, whisking back into the milk any skin that forms. Simmer until the milk has reduced to a third of the volume, about 35 minutes. There will be a slight caramel smell. Remove the pan from the heat and add the sugar, stirring until it has dissolved. Pour the mixture into another bowl to cool, then cover and refrigerate it for several hours to allow the flavours to blend.

Strain the mixture, stirring it through a sieve, then stir in the cream, ground almonds and kewra essence, if using.

Pour the mixture into your ice-lolly moulds, leaving 5mm at the top to allow the mixture to expand when it freezes. Sprinkle the chopped pistachios over the top. Insert the lolly sticks and freeze. (See page 22 for the complete procedure.)

CEREAL MILK

Inspired by the famous cereal-milk soft serve that created a frenzy in New York City, we've created our own version by freezing Lily's morning cereal onto a stick and it was quite a hit! You can experiment yourself and use your preferred cereals and we know you'll agree it will taste even better in this frozen form.

- 300ml whole milk
- 250ml double cream
- 30g your favourite breakfast cereal (we like Cheerios), plus extra to drop into the moulds
- 1 ripe banana, cut into 2-cm slices
- 5-6 tablespoons honey or maple syrup

Mix all the ingredients together in a bowl, cover and refrigerate overnight to allow the liquid to take on that unmistakably delicious cereal taste.

The next day, put the steeped mixture in a food processor and blend until smooth.

Pour the mixture into your ice-lolly moulds, and drop in some extra pieces of cereal. Leave 5mm at the top to allow the mixture to expand when it freezes. Insert the lolly sticks and freeze. (See page 22 for the complete procedure.)

ICE KITCHEN

NEW YORK BLACK & WHITE

We make this vanilla lolly into the 'New York Black & White' by dipping half of it in dark and half in white chocolate in homage to the much loved New York black and white cookie. You can tell how good an ice cream chef is by how good their vanilla ice cream tastes.

For the vanilla:
- 400ml whole milk
- 200ml double cream
- 120g granulated sugar
- a pinch of salt
- 1 vanilla pod
- 4 egg yolks

For the dipping chocolate:
- 100g white chocolate
- 100g dark chocolate
- 2 tablespoons vegetable oil

Put the milk, cream, sugar and salt in a saucepan over a low heat. Cut along the vanilla pod and scrape the seeds out into the pan and add the pod too. Put the egg yolks in a heatproof bowl and briefly whisk. When the milk starts to simmer, take it off the heat and gradually add a ladleful into the egg mixture, whisking well. Gradually add 2 more ladles while whisking, then pour back into the pan. Heat over a low-medium heat, stirring, until thickened enough to easily coat the back of a wooden spoon. Do not let it boil. Pour it immediately through a fine sieve into a bowl. Put the vanilla pod back into the custard. Allow the mixture to cool, then refrigerate for 2 hours or overnight to thicken. Pull out the vanilla pod and scrape the remaining seeds into the custard.

Pour the mixture into your ice-lolly moulds, leaving 5mm at the top to allow the mixture to expand when it freezes. Insert the lolly sticks and freeze. (See page 22 for the complete procedure.) To dip the lollies in the white and dark chocolates, see page 20.

CARAMEL CHOCOLATE

This is Cesar's indulgent recipe for a caramel lolly which is great as it is, but even better dipped in chocolate and almonds.

- 175g granulated sugar
- 500ml whole milk
- 250ml double cream
- 3 egg yolks
- ~~¼ teaspoon vanilla extract~~
- a pinch of salt

Place a heavy saucepan over a medium heat. Once hot, pour the sugar in and shake the pan, stirring with a wooden spoon until the sugar has melted. When the sugar starts to colour, it will caramelise and the temperature will rise very quickly, so watch it! Do not burn it or it will become bitter. As soon as it's golden amber, remove the pan from the heat. Add the milk and cream straightaway, but be very careful because it will splutter and spit. Put back over the heat and bring to a simmer, stirring to dissolve the hardened caramel.

In a large bowl, briefly whisk together the egg yolks, vanilla and salt. Remove the pan from the heat and gradually whisk the hot caramel into the eggs, then transfer everything back into the pan. Heat again over a medium heat, stirring constantly until the mixture thickens enough to easily coat the back of a wooden spoon. Do not let it boil! Strain the mixture into a clean bowl and place the bowl over ice to cool it quickly. Now refrigerate it until chilled.

Pour the mixture into your ice-lolly moulds, leaving 5mm at the top to allow the mixture to expand when it freezes. Insert the lolly sticks and freeze. (See page 22 for the complete procedure.) To cap the frozen lollies with chocolate, see page 20, adding chopped almonds to the melted chocolate.

ICE KITCHEN

MEXICAN CHOCOLATE

Inspired by the Aztecs' chocolate and chilli drink, this is an intriguing and moreish combination that we can't get enough of.

- 500ml whole milk
- 250ml double cream
- 1 cinnamon stick, broken up
- 3-5 generous pinches of cayenne pepper,
  plus optional extra to sprinkle on the lollies
- 150g dark chocolate, finely chopped
- 65g granulated sugar

Put the milk, cream, cinnamon stick and cayenne pepper in a medium saucepan and bring to a simmer. Simmer for 5 minutes. Remove the pan from the heat, add the chocolate and sugar and stir until well blended and creamy.

Set the mixture aside to cool and to allow the flavours to infuse. The longer it sits, the smoother and creamier your lolly will be. We sometimes let it sit overnight.

Strain the mixture through a fine sieve, then pour it into your ice-lolly moulds, leaving 5mm at the top to allow the mixture to expand when it freezes. Insert the lolly sticks and freeze. (See page 22 for the complete procedure.) Sprinkle just a tiny bit of extra cayenne pepper on the frozen lollies, if you like.

CHOCOLATE & VANILLA SWIRL

Sicilians use cornflour as a thickener in their ice cream – it allows the flavours to shine through and it gives a good texture. Here we use it to add a nice chewy bite to the lolly. If you like a deeper chocolate, use the cocoa powder in addition to the dark chocolate.

- 500ml whole milk
- 20g cornflour
- 250ml double cream
- 2 teaspoons vanilla extract
- 6 tablespoons granulated sugar
- 100g dark chocolate, finely chopped
- 4 teaspoons unsweetened cocoa powder mixed with 3 tablespoons hot water (optional)

Put 3 tablespoons of the milk in a small bowl and mix in the cornflour to form a smooth paste. Pour the remaining milk and the cream in a medium saucepan and heat until just about to simmer, then stir in the cornflour paste. Stir constantly until the mixture starts to thicken and bubble. Allow to thicken, stirring, for a further 2 minutes.

Pour the mixture through a fine sieve and divide between 2 bowls. Stir half the vanilla and 4 tablespoons of the sugar into one bowl; and stir the remaining vanilla and remaining sugar plus the chocolate into the second bowl until smooth and well blended. If you are using the cocoa powder mixture, stir it into the chocolate bowl. Allow the mixtures to cool to room temperature.

Spoon alternate vanilla and chocolate layers in your ice-lolly moulds, leaving 5mm at the top to allow the mixture to expand when it freezes. Insert lolly sticks and freeze. (See page 22 for the complete procedure.)

ICE KITCHEN

CHOCOLATE

This recipe gives you the perfect chocolate lolly that you can enjoy - pure and simple. It can also be transformed with other flavourings, such as orange, rosemary, rose or coffee (see Variations below).

8-10

- 500ml whole milk
- 250ml double cream
- 150g good-quality dark chocolate, finely chopped
- 65-75g granulated sugar (depending on the sweetness of your chocolate)
- 2 teaspoons vanilla extract

Put the milk and cream in a saucepan and bring to a simmer. Remove the pan from the heat, add the chocolate and sugar and stir until well blended and creamy. Stir in the vanilla. Set the mixture aside to cool. The longer it sits, the smoother and creamier your lolly will be.

Pour the mixture into your ice-lolly moulds, leaving 5mm at the top to allow the mixture to expand when it freezes. Insert the lolly sticks and freeze. (See page 22 for the complete procedure.)

If you like you can artfully drip some melted dark chocolate over the lolly (see page 20 for help with melting chocolate).

Variations:
For orange chocolate, add 2 teaspoons finely grated orange zest; for rose chocolate, add 2 teaspoons rose water; for rosemary chocolate, add a few sprigs of fresh rosemary to the milk as it simmers and pull them out just before freezing. For those who love mocha, stir in 2 teaspoons instant coffee at the same time as the chocolate.

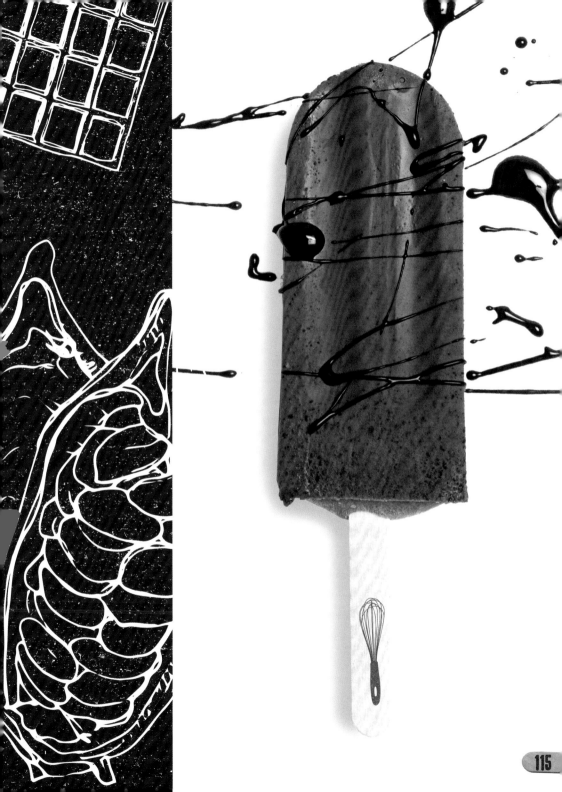

CAPPUCCINO

Use really fresh, dark roast coffee and make it extra strong for this cappuccino-on-a-stick. We use a ceramic coffee dripper with a paper cone right over a cup. If you have an espresso machine, that's even better.

 8-10

- 60g granulated sugar
- 500ml freshly brewed, extra strong coffee
- 250ml whipping cream
- 1-2 tablespoons caster sugar
- 1-2 drops of vanilla extract (optional)
- cocoa powder, ground cinnamon, or grated nutmeg to sprinkle on the lollies

Add the granulated sugar to the freshly brewed coffee and stir until the sugar has dissolved. Stir in half the cream until it's well blended.

Put the remaining cream, caster sugar and vanilla, if using, in a bowl and beat until slightly firm.

Pour the coffee mixture into your ice-lolly moulds - there should be some room left for the cream. Spoon the cream on top, leaving 5mm at the top to allow the mixture to expand when it freezes. Insert the lolly sticks and freeze. (See page 22 for the complete procedure.) Sprinkle cocoa powder, ground cinnamon or grated nutmeg over the frozen lollies, if you like.

VIETNAMESE COFFEE

As young artists in New York, we used to go around the corner to a Vietnamese restaurant called Nha Trang in Chinatown for cheap and delicious meals. They used to bring each of us a cup with sweet condensed milk in the bottom and then brewed a coffee through a small metal filter individually over each cup. The whole ceremony made a big impression. Here it is, on a stick. To brew the strong coffee needed for this lolly, we use a paper filter directly over a cup and load it with coffee grounds. You'll be flying.

- 150ml sweetened condensed milk
- 500ml freshly brewed, extra strong coffee (the very strongest you can make!)
- 100ml double cream

Put the condensed milk into a bowl and pour the freshly brewed coffee and the cream over it. Mix until completely blended.

Pour the mixture into your ice-lolly moulds, leaving 5mm at the top to allow the mixture to expand when it freezes. Insert the lolly sticks and freeze. (See page 22 for the complete procedure.)

EARL GREY

Earl Grey, the British prime minister in the 1830s, reportedly received this blend of tea as a gift from a Chinese Mandarin. The tea is distinctively scented with the oil of the bergamot orange.

- 500ml whole milk
- 20g cornflour
- 250ml double cream
- 120g granulated sugar
- 5 teaspoons Earl Grey tea leaves
- 1 teaspoon vanilla extract (optional)

Put 3 tablespoons of the milk in a small bowl and mix in the cornflour to form a smooth paste. Pour the remaining milk, the cream and sugar in a medium saucepan and heat until just about to boil, remove the pan from the heat and stir in the tea leaves. Allow to steep for 5 minutes.

Stir in the cornflour paste and return the pan to the heat. Stir constantly until the mixture starts to thicken and bubble. Allow to thicken, stirring constantly, for a further 2 minutes.

Pour the mixture through a fine sieve, pressing down on the leaves with the back of a spoon to extract the flavour. Stir in the vanilla, if using, and allow to cool to room temperature.

Pour the mixture into your ice-lolly moulds, leaving 5mm at the top to allow the mixture to expand when it freezes. Insert the lolly sticks and freeze. (See page 22 for the complete procedure.)

Variation:
You can substitute another highly fragrant tea leaf for the Earl Grey.

ICE KITCHEN

CUCUMBER & LIME

This refreshing and intense lolly is perfect for a break during a sweltering day or for a warm summer evening outside. The skin of the cucumber is where the nutrients are stored and is also what gives this lolly its jade green colour, so don't remove it!

8-10

- 1 large English cucumber, rinsed
- 250ml water
- 85ml freshly squeezed lime juice (from about 2-3 limes)
- 100g granulated sugar

Leave the skin on the cucumber. Cut off the ends and slice the cucumber thickly. Put the cucumber and water in a food processor and blend to a fine purée.

Strain the purée through a fine sieve and add the lime juice and sugar. Stir until the sugar has dissolved.

Pour the mixture into your ice-lolly moulds, leaving 5mm at the top to allow the mixture to expand when it freezes. Insert the lolly sticks and freeze. (See page 22 for the complete procedure.)

BEETROOT & SOUR CREAM

Be prepared for a pair of beautifully stained magenta lips after eating this! This Russian-inspired lolly is also full of health benefits. It's easiest to use fresh shop-bought beetroot juice but you can make your own, of course. If you do, be sure to keep the skins on when you run them through the juicer, since that is where most of the nutrients are stored.

 8-10

- 500ml fresh beetroot juice
- 2 tablespoons freshly squeezed lemon juice
- 2 tablespoons caster sugar
- 250ml sour cream

Mix together the beetroot and lemon juices and sugar. Stir until the sugar has dissolved. Stir in the sour cream until well blended.

Pour the mixture into your ice-lolly moulds, leaving 5mm at the top to allow the mixture to expand when it freezes. Insert the lolly sticks and freeze. (See page 22 for the complete procedure.)

INDEX

ACKNOWLEDGEMENTS

We'd like to thank everyone at Quadrille for the idea of making this book and giving us so much freedom to do it: Ed and Simon for their enthusiasm and vision, Jane for her wise guidance throughout, Helen for her exceptional eye, Gemma for making it look this beautiful, and Céline for her sensitive editing. Special thanks to Lizzy Kremer, our awesome agent.

Thank you, Lily, for being the biggest inspiration and for being our ultimate taste tester. We thank Claudia who taught us the pleasures of cooking and who is always there for us; Paul for his belief and encouragement to always follow our dreams and to shoot from the hip; Peggy for getting caught up in this lolly madness, and for all her hard work. A big thank you to Peter for designing the book and striking cover, his girlfriend Divya Scialo for helping with line illustrations, and our friend Adam Slama for photographing all the lollies so beautifully.

A massive thank you to Simon and Ros for helping to set up the Ice Kitchen at their home last year and making it all possible, and for putting up with all the endless crates of fruit.

Special thanks to Sybil for her generous spirit; Tom for the website, Chantal for her sound advice; and our families and Gemma and Terry for being the lolly guinea pigs, even when they didn't turn out so well and didn't make it into the book. Thank you all for your love and support.